THE
MARTIAL ARTS

THE MARTIAL ARTS

by Ken Reisberg

FRANKLIN WATTS
NEW YORK | LONDON | TORONTO | 1979
A FIRST BOOK

OPPOSITE TITLE PAGE: A JUDO BODY DROP.

Cover photograph by Clara Spain

Photographs courtesy of Annan Photo Features: pp.
ii and 25 (Hughes); Photo Trends: pp. 16 (XSF), 23
(Colin Davey) 37, and 43; United Press International:
pp. 34 and 70; and Japan National Tourist Organi-
zation: pp. 48, 55, and 58.

Drawings by Elliott Ivenbaum

Library of Congress Cataloging in Publication Data

Reisberg, Ken.
The martial arts.

(A First book)
Bibliography: p.
Includes index.
SUMMARY: Presents a history of the martial arts
and describes the individual disciplines stressing
the value of martial arts training as a method of
building physical and spiritual strength.
1.   Hand-to-hand fighting, Oriental—Juvenile litera-
ture. [1. Martial arts.   2.   Hand-to-hand fighting, Oriental] I. Title.
GV1112.R44   796.8'15   79–10506
            ISBN 0–531–04077–1

Contents

Dedicated to the advancement
of international good will
through the study of martial arts

Preface

The first time I entered a training school for the martial arts, I was only nine years old. The school, or dojo as I later learned it was called, was located inside a large hall. There was no furniture. All the walls except one were bare. On that wall hung a huge piece of rectangular white cloth with a bright red circle painted in the middle and beside it a collection of the most unusual looking objects I had ever seen. The cloth, I was told, was the national flag of Japan. The objects were weapons of every kind imaginable.

There were about twenty men, women, and children inside the dojo. Each was dressed in a loose-fitting, two-piece white uniform that had a belt tied around at the waist. The instructor, or sensei as he was called, wore a black belt. He called the class to order. The students lined up shoulder to shoulder, with those wearing belts of the same shade standing together. At the direction of the sensei, the class dropped down to their knees and bowed in unison, first to the flag, then to the sensei. The class remained still for many moments. Following this period of silent meditation, the class was led through a number of strenuous stretching exercises. The weapons were then removed from the wall and the students divided into small groups.

In the months that followed, I would enroll in my first karate class and be taught many things. What I would learn would leave me forever fascinated with the study of the martial arts.

AUTHOR'S NOTE In writing this book, I have conferred with a number of notable martial artists, including Master Fung Yi, who is a personal acquaintance of the author and teacher to the late kung-fu star Bruce Lee. Master Yi was also chief inspector of Chinese police in Shanghai and speaks fluent Chinese, Japanese, Malaysian, and English. He has himself acted in the Bruce Lee movie called *Fists of Fury* (later renamed *The Chinese Connection*) alongside his former student. I wish to give special thanks to Mr. Yi and to all the other martial artists who assisted in making this book all that it was intended to be.

The History and Meaning of the Martial Arts

The **martial arts** are fighting forms designed especially for self-defense. They are also exciting, competitive sports that promote health, strength, and a sense of fair play.

The goal of martial arts training is the achievement of mental, physical, and spiritual strength. When properly studied, one develops an alertness that can prove invaluable in overcoming physically threatening situations.

The people who long ago inhabited the portion of the Asian continent known as the Far East invented the martial arts. They were a people small of stature and slight of build. Because they were constantly under threat of attack from neighboring hostile clans or warring nations, a knowledge of self-defense was basic to their survival. Realizing how effective the right weapons could be against a more formidable opponent, the

Oriental peoples placed great importance on proper weapon handling.

As time passed, systems of combat were devised so that each weapon could be used with utmost effectiveness. A great deal of training was necessary to learn the basic **sparring** techniques of each weapon. Still more time was needed to become expert at them. Success in battle was no longer simply a matter of who was the stronger. The best trained and most highly skilled warrior was now the most likely victor. The ability to prevail in battle against superior numbers and strength became thought of as an art. The experts of combat were the **grand masters** of the martial arts.

THE GRAND MASTERS

These seemingly invincible men lived their lives according to certain beliefs of the Buddhist religion. In the way of **Zen Buddhism,** life was holy and force was justified in defending it. However, the grand masters used physical force only for self-defense and only then as a last resort.

To insure that their lethal methods of combat would not be used by others with less noble motives, the grand masters led a very secretive life. For countless years the martial arts remained a treasured secret. Only a relatively few were fortunate enough to be chosen to share in the secret of the martial arts. Those chosen were also followers of Zen and had distinguished themselves by their character and devotion. Each disciple would be cautioned to use his warring skills only in self-defense. Later, however, some masters would begin to use their special training to defend their lands or the property of other townsmen or to aid those to whom they owed allegiance. These men would become the most vivid personalities in the history of warfare. They would also become more loved and more feared than any other soldier throughout history. These men would come to be known by the name **samurai.**

THE SAMURAI WARRIOR

The life of the samurai was one of integrity and duty. Integrity was the way of life for the samurai, duty was his purpose for living. The deeds of the samurai were marked by his outstanding courage. It was this combination of courage and integrity that won the samurai the respect of all, friend and foe alike. There was never a mission too great for the samurai warrior, provided its cause was just. When in combat, the samurai would fight to the death. He would never retreat and never compromise, as for him these would be signs of weakness. Above all, the samurai would never disgrace those who had put their trust in him. In battle there was no single opponent to be found that could match him. This would be true whether the weapon used was a spear, chain, or sword.

It was the sword of the samurai, however, that was his most prized possession. At times, it was his only possession. The samurai could use his sword with the quickness of a magician and the precision of a master surgeon. Fashioned from heavy steel, the samurai sword was unbreakable and nearly unbeatable in the hands of its owner. The samurai sword came to be regarded as a symbol of nobility. Today, original sam-

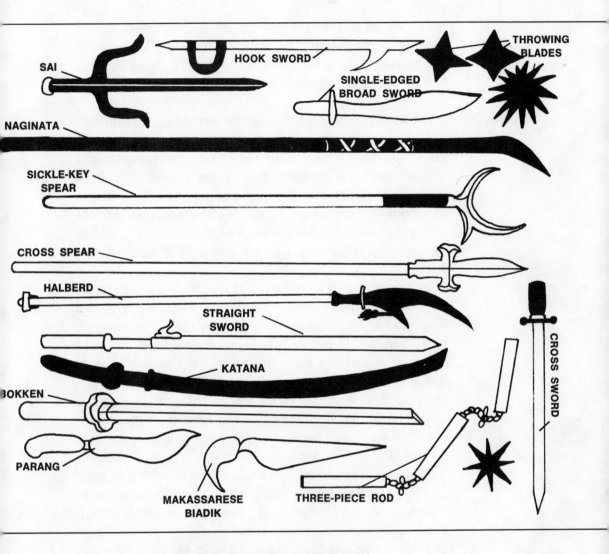

SAI

HOOK SWORD

THROWING BLADES

SINGLE-EDGED BROAD SWORD

NAGINATA

SICKLE-KEY SPEAR

CROSS SPEAR

HALBERD

STRAIGHT SWORD

KATANA

BOKKEN

CROSS SWORD

PARANG

MAKASSARESE BIADIK

THREE-PIECE ROD

Left: the samurai may have been the most loved and most feared soldier in history. Above: samurai weapons

urai swords are much sought after and rarely found outside of museums. The sight of the samurai sword in Japan, even today, brings to mind the most glorious era in that country's history, "the days of the samurai."

BUSHIDO   **Bushido** was most probably the greatest contribution of the samurai warrior. Bushido was the code of conduct that gave meaning to the life of the samurai and afterward to the people of later-day Japan. The term bushido, meaning literally "the ways of the knighthood," has come to represent many of the traditional beliefs and customs of feudal Japan. For this reason, bushido has often been spoken of as being "the soul of Old Japan."

Bushido was, and remains today, a strong influence in martial arts training. Traditional customs are still observed inside the martial arts school. The training hall itself is still called a **dojo,** as it has been for centuries. The uniform worn by the student of martial arts today resembles in many ways the **kimono** of the original samurai warrior. The practice of removing one's shoes before entering the training area is another custom that has been passed down through the ages. This particular custom arose while the fighting arts were taught by the grand masters within the confines of their temples. During those times it was forbidden to wear shoes or slippers while in prayer or even when eating. Bowing is another polite formality unique to the sport of martial arts. At first, men and women were required to bow only to elders and to certain people of distinction as an expression of deep respect. Today, students bow while in the dojo to their **sensei** (teacher) and to their opponent before and after every match or contest.

THE SECRET REVEALED The increased use of firearms during the mid-nineteenth century resulted in a major revolution in the art of warfare. The military value of firepower as compared to conventional weapons became well recognized. Even the heroic samurai warrior, who was unequaled in hand-to-hand combat, was no match against men armed with these new high-powered weapons. The art of warfare was rapidly changing from a contest between men of opposing armies into a battle of machines. The sword had become a weapon of a past era. In 1878, the **Meiji** government of Japan announced a ban against the wearing or use of swords. Interest in the fighting arts began to suffer a steady period of decline. The secret of the martial arts, however, remained alive in the hearts and minds of a chosen few.

Several years following the Meiji Edict of 1878, a group of dedicated teachers of self-defense successfully petitioned their new government to allow them to hold public exhibitions of their fighting skills. Demonstrations were staged in the use of ancient weaponry and various styles of unarmed combat. These exhibitions were well received. Renewed enthusiasm for the study of the martial arts resulted. Under pressure from the masses, the new government allowed these expert teachers to open schools for martial arts training. These dojos were open to men and women from every social class. No more were the secrets of the fighting arts in the hands of a select few.

THE WORLD TAKES NOTICE

The world first took notice of the value of the martial arts during the Second World War. At that time, the United States and Japan were at war with each other. Much of the fighting between these two countries took place in the jungle islands off the coast of Japan. It was here that the Japanese soldier was able to demonstrate to the U.S. high command the effectiveness of the ancient Oriental fighting arts. Despite a great difference in size, the Japanese soldier was nevertheless capable of defeating the taller and stronger American leathernecks in hand-to-hand combat. The marines, who were themselves noted for their bravery, came to respect and admire the fighting abilities of the smaller Oriental soldier. With the aid of the news media, it wasn't long before the martial arts came to be regarded as the "ultimate" methods of self-defense. Many countries adopted the Oriental fighting techniques of unarmed combat for use in training their own recruits. In the United States, England, and Canada, special military divisions were formed that received intense expert training in the martial arts. These combat units became as familiar to the average person as Commandos, Special Forces, and later, Green Berets.

Besides their distinction as the ultimate methods of self-defense, the ancient fighting forms also soon became recognized as highly competitive sports. Martial arts tournaments are held today in every major city in the world. In 1964 the martial arts succeeded in gaining entry into the international Olympic Games. This is considered to be the highest tribute that can be bestowed upon any sport. The art of **judo** is now a permanent event of the athletic program of the summer Olympics. Today, millions of people the world over practice the martial arts. These include people in business, office workers, homemakers, students, and young children. Some famous people who studied the martial arts include the late President Theodore Roosevelt, the late Elvis Presley, Steve McQueen, Diana Rigg, James Garner, William Shatner, Jimmy Connors, and Carol Lawrence.

The Dojo

This book will help you in getting started in the martial arts. In fact, after reading this book from cover to cover, you might even know more about the martial arts than students who have already spent weeks or months at practice. However, you cannot become proficient in the execution of the martial arts without proper coaching, training, and facilities. Only the dojo can offer you all this.

Dojo is a Japanese word that means "fencing hall." In modern times, however, a dojo has come to represent any hall where any of the martial arts are practiced. These training halls vary widely in appearance and size. A dojo may be a converted house, studio, loft, or storefront. Your local classified directory is an excellent source in locating the dojos in your neighborhood.

CHOOSING A DOJO   If you make your home in a big city you should have no problem finding a number of dojos from which to choose. On the other hand, if you live in a small town, you probably will not be able to be quite as selective. Nowadays, though, because of their tremendous popularity, you can always find a place to learn the martial arts. Besides being taught in dojos, courses in the Oriental fighting sports are now offered in community centers, after-school programs, camps, and clubs.

A visit to a martial arts practice hall is a must, regardless of whether or not you intend to join. Watching the "secret" arts of self-defense at work will be an unforgettable experience. Should you decide to study one of the martial arts, it would be wise to visit several of the dojos in your area. You will notice that besides their differences in appearance, there will be variations in the types of martial arts that are studied. You will also learn how the methods of teaching vary from school to school. To reach your fullest potential in the martial arts, you must begin by carefully choosing a reputable club. Finding answers to the following question should help you make a good choice.

Do other boys and girls my age belong?
Is the membership fee reasonable (compared to others in the area)?
Are the class hours convenient?
Can I use the dojo to practice without formal instruction?
Do the students make an effort to help one another?
Is discipline maintained in the training hall?

Does the dojo participate in contests with other clubs? Do the students appear involved and eager to learn? Are class sizes small enough to allow for some individual attention?

A reputable club will always welcome visitors to come and watch a class in progress. It will be happy to take time to answer all your questions and sometimes will even invite you to a free trial lesson without obligation. The sensei will have earned his or her degree from a recognized martial arts association. A dojo with a good reputation may often have a waiting list for beginners' classes. If this is the case, put your name down, because your patience will be well rewarded.

Beware of clubs that insist upon you or your parents signing contracts that require large deposits and long-term membership commitments. These dojos are more interested in making money than in teaching the martial arts. Sometimes these schools will "guarantee" you a black belt, the highest rank, after only one year of study. A reputable instructor would never make such a promise.

Judo: "The Gentle Way"

In Japan during the middle of the last century lived a small boy named Jigoro Kano. Like other boys and girls his age, he loved to hear the legends of the great "bushi" and how they walked deliberately and fearlessly into the face of danger. When Jigoro was a teenager, he was privileged to study the ancient fighting arts under the most learned teachers of his day. He was a perfect student and earned the rank of expert in **jiujitsu,** the deadly art of unarmed combat. Jigoro still kept on with his formal schooling and later became an educator himself.

One day, Dr. Jigoro Kano had an inspiration. He thought, why couldn't the ancient fighting forms be taught as competitive sports? Dr. Kano opened his own school, called the **Kodokan,** for that purpose. He borrowed the best techniques of several of the ancient

arts of unarmed combat and combined them into one. To distinguish his new sport from other Oriental arts, Dr. Kano called it judo. The rest of his life was spent in promoting judo as an international sport.

Due to Dr. Kano's efforts, judo is now practiced in every civilized country in the world. In the United States judo is recognized by the Amateur Athletic Union, the largest sports body in the country. Judo is also included in the Pan American and Olympic Games. All this is now a reality due to the insight and inspiration of one man, Dr. Jigoro Kano, the founding father of the art of judo.

THE ART OF JUDO

Judo is more than a sport and more than a means of self-defense. Judo is an art. The art of judo involves the ability to use the least amount of effort to overcome the greatest amount of force. The principles that form the basis of the art of judo are maximum efficiency, minimum effort, and mutual aid. A judo master will use any part of his or her body to off-balance an opponent. In judo, hitting, kicking, and striking are strictly forbidden. In fact, the word judo literally means "the gentle way." Instead of powerful blows, the **judoka** throws the adversary and applies holds to render him or her helpless. In judo, the training methods and equipment used are designed to prevent accidental injury.

Judo—the *gentle* way? Here a hip throw is being performed by a beginning judoka.

The Judo Mat In practicing judo, every move should be performed on a mat. In the dojo, this mat is usually large enough to cover most of the inside floor area. The construction of judo mats vary. They can be filled with rice, rubber, or foam. Some popular judo mats are hollow with canvas tops and closely resemble boxing rings. There are never any ropes, however, surrounding the judo mat. A good judo mat will be at least several inches (about 5 cm) thick and be able to offset the impact of the hardest fall.

If you can't get to a dojo and still want to practice judo, gym mats can be made to substitute for standard judo mats. When practicing on your own, first make certain that there is enough matted area to safely fall upon. When you practice judo, you should always dress for the activity.

The Judo Gi Judo is always performed barefoot. The standard uniform used in judo is called a **gi.** This gi consists of a loose-fitting jacket and pants made from reinforced heavy cotton. You can purchase your gi at the dojo or order it from a martial arts catalog. With proper care, your gi will last through many months and even years of steady use. It is generally advisable to order a gi one size larger than normal to allow for shrinkage. Included with the gi is a long white cotton belt about 7 feet (2.1 m) long, which is wrapped twice around at the waist and fitted into a square knot. The shade of the uniform belt has a special meaning.

The Judo Ranks The belt you wear represents your degree of proficiency in judo. Belts are awarded for experience,

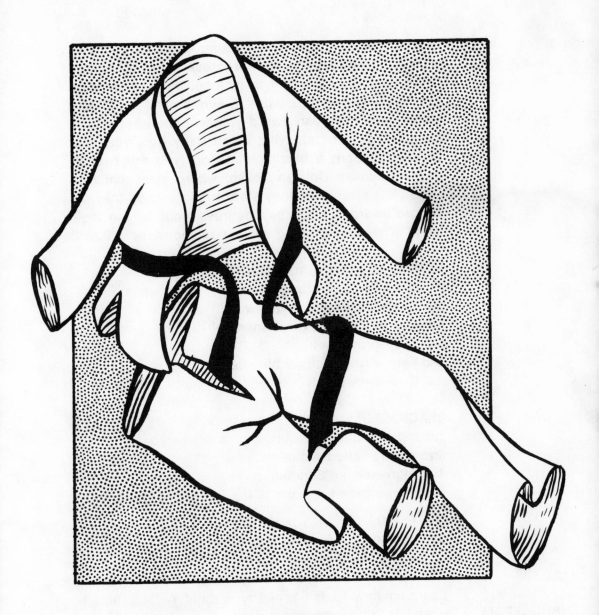

The judo gi.

technical knowledge, and fighting ability. Beginners start with white belts and progress through various "classes" called **kyu** to the black belt rank called **dan.** The standard belts are white, green, brown, and black. Many clubs now also award yellow, orange, and blue belts. If you start studying at an early age, you may be able to earn a black belt before you are twenty. In the Kodokan Dojo in Tokyo, where many children join at the same time they start public school, they often are awarded black belt degrees while still in their teens. The judo grading system is shown as follows:

RANKS BELOW BLACK BELT
6th Kyu—white belt (beginner)
5th Kyu—white belt (or yellow belt)
4th Kyu—green belt (or orange belt)
3rd Kyu—brown belt
2nd Kyu—brown belt (or blue belt)
1st Kyu—brown belt

BLACK BELTS
1st degree called Shodan
2nd degree called Nidan
3rd degree called Sandan
4th degree called Yondan

NOTE: Ranks above Yondan are very rare and are only awarded for exceptional contribution to the sport of judo.

UKEMI (BREAKFALLS) Learning how to fall properly without getting hurt is useful in all sports and practical in everyday life. In judo, where "players" are almost always trying to throw one another, learning the right way to fall is absolutely essential. You cannot progress in other judo skills before learning **ukemi**. In falling—forward, backward, or sideward—the arms are most useful in minimizing the impact of the fall. Referring to the figures shown, notice how, in practicing breakfalls, the arms slam down hard upon the mat and how the head is tucked in to prevent it from hitting the ground. When you can fall without fear from any position you will be ready to practice judo with a friend.

TORI AND UKE

In judo the player who is the aggressor is called **tori.** The player who is thrown or otherwise subdued is called **uke.** In judo you must learn to be both tori and uke eventually.

TRAINING METHODS

Uchikomi (form practice): To practice newly learned skills, uke cooperates by not fully resisting tori and allowing himself or herself to be thrown. This helps tori work on style and accuracy.

Randori (free-standing exercise): Partners practice by each trying to throw the other cleanly to the mat. Full resistance is applied by both players in randori.

Newaza (freestyle floor exercise): Partners practice hold downs, armlocks, and advanced choking techniques on the mat.

Shiai (contest): A match between two judo players overseen by a referee and two judges. The shiai is the true test of one's ability. The object in a shiai is to be the first player to score a point, called **ippon,** by executing a clean throw, hold down, or armlock.

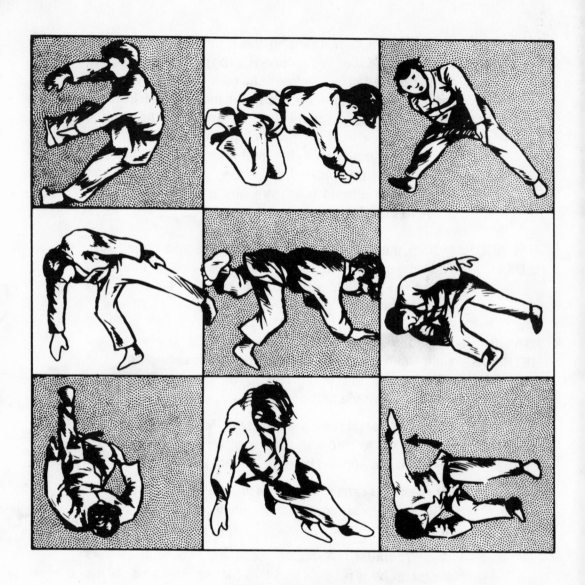

Above: judo breakfalls.
Right: a judo class
in a convent school.

NAGE WAZA (THROWING TECHNIQUES)

A successful judo throw requires timing, coordination, and balance. Balance is the fundamental principle of judo. The object in all judo throws is to offset your opponent's balance while maintaining your own. The Japanese have a special name for this skill; they call it **kuzushi.** Sometimes, a person is already off balance and is an easy target for a throw. Many times, however, it is necessary to lead an opponent off-balance by pulling or pushing him or her in the direction of an attempted throw. This is why judokas are constantly seen grabbing at each other's uniforms.

As you study judo you will learn many different types of throws. The **nage waza** or throwing techniques you will learn are generally divided into four separate groupings, shown in the illustrations. It takes years of practice to master all of the combinations of throws included in each of these groupings. In tournament play, however, it takes only one completed throw to win a match. The reason for this rule is that if a person who was unfamiliar with the proper method of falling was to be flung onto a hard surface, he or she would be at least momentarily paralyzed. The judo masters called **shihans** devote their lives toward perfecting all the throws that comprise judo, but you can learn a few basic throws in only a short time.

OSAE KOMI WAZA (GROUNDWORK)

During a typical judo match, one or both players often fall to the mat without being properly thrown. When this occurs the contest is allowed to continue. More

**A shoulder throw
during a judo match.**

HIP THROW

LEG THROW

SHOULDER THROW

ANKLE THROW

Judo throws

Groundwork in judo

than half of judo is played on the mat. The idea in matwork, or groundwork as it is commonly called, is to score a point by holding your opponent down for thirty seconds. This is done by locking the opponent in a hold from which he or she cannot escape. Judo players must use special caution not to seriously hurt each other on the mat. They must be alert to every movement of their opponent. Whenever a player taps twice on the mat with either arms or legs, the other player must release his or her grip immediately. A player may also voluntarily stop the match by calling out the word **Mattai!** This means "Let go—I give up!" In Judo, players never try to purposely hurt each other. Instead, they have more fun doing it "the gentle way."

Karate:
"The Empty Hand"

Around the year 500 A.D. lived an Indian monk named Bhodidharma who was revered as one of the greatest men of his time. Bhodidharma was credited as having been the founder of Zen Buddhism and the martial art form of **karate.** Like many great people throughout history, Bhodidharma was strongly committed to an unselfish goal. His ambition was to share his knowledge and skill with the Buddhist monks of China.

The journey from India to China was a long, arduous, and very dangerous one. For one person to set forth alone upon such a journey was unthinkable. Bhodidharma, however, was no ordinary man. He began his self-chosen crusade with only his strong will and determination to sustain him. The obstacles that stood in his way were very real and threatening. One major problem that confronted him were the gangs of armed bandits who roamed the countryside. As a holy man, Bhodidharma would not allow himself to carry any weapon, even for self-protection. The only defense he had against these armed bandit gangs were his "empty hands" and his knowledge of karate. These things alone were responsible for saving the life of the Indian monk on several occasions. When Bhodidharma at last arrived at his destination, the **Shaolin-Szu** monastery, he recounted his experiences and all he had learned. The Chinese monks were highly impressed and adopted his martial art discipline of karate for their own self-defense.

KARATE IN OKINAWA

Okinawa is an island located midway between the mainlands of China and Japan. Because of its small size and strategic location, Okinawa was frequently subject to foreign attack. In the seventeenth century, the Japanese successfully invaded the island. All weapons on the island were confiscated. But still the people would not give up the desire to regain their freedom. Years before, the emptyhanded art of self-defense had been introduced in Okinawa. Those who knew it were determined, in spite of the consequences, to teach it to their fellow countrymen. They hoped that this would lift the spirits of the people and inflame their desire for freedom. The Japanese rulers were informed of this secret plan. Their reaction to this information, however, was a complete surprise. They were more curious than angry. They wondered how effective karate would be against their own armed and unarmed methods of combat. To determine this, they arranged matches between their own soldiers and the Okinawan karate instructors. The Okinawans greatly impressed the Japanese with their ability in hand-to-hand combat.

FUNAKOSHI AND MODERN KARATE

Gichin Funakoshi was the person who was most instrumental in fostering interest in karate in Japan. This native Okinawan karate teacher demonstrated an exceptional talent in the art of unarmed combat. His name and reputation came to be known throughout the island. There were countless men who challenged him, but none who could beat him. So very impressive was Funakoshi in these matches that he was invited to visit the imperial palace in Japan in 1917 to demonstrate this "new" martial art. When he first arrived, many people were skeptical of the effectiveness of karate and doubtful of Funakoshi's own ability. This was partly because of his physical appearance. Funakoshi was thin and stood only 5 feet 1 inch (1.52 m) in height! Compared to the powerfully built Japanese wrestlers or even the typical citizen he looked anything but fearsome. After observing him in contests, however, the image of Funakoshi quickly changed. People came to respect him and the effectiveness of his novel martial art. Because of his reputation the popularity of karate spread throughout Japan. When Funakoshi died, a monument was erected in his memory. Today he is remembered as the father of modern karate.

KARATE IN THE NORTHERN HEMISPHERE

The first karate schools in the continental United States were opened on the West Coast. Originally, club membership was limited to Oriental people who had immigrated to that part of the country. In time, though, karate schools began to materialize in urban communities all over the continent. With a strong foothold in the cities, karate dojos then branched out into the less congested suburbs. As this pattern of development continued in North America, the interest in karate in Europe was also on the upswing. People came to realize the overall value of karate in everyday living. There were, however, significant differences in the styles of karate that became popular.

STYLES OF KARATE There are a number of styles of karate taught today. While almost every style claims to be superior, in fairness all have much to offer. As a beginner, you should be familiar with the fundamental characteristics of these major styles of teaching:

Shotokan After his formal retirement from competition, Funakoshi, the great master, opened a dojo in Tokyo, Japan. His students named it **Shotokan.** Shoto was a nickname the students had for their master teacher. Kan is a Japanese word meaning school. Shotokan developed into the most popular western style of karate. Shotokan is considered a hard form of karate that stresses maximum power through straight and direct blows.

Goju Chojun Miyagi, another Okinawan, is credited as being the originator of **goju.** This form is regarded as a "hard and soft" style of karate. Those who study goju consider it the best system of karate because it concurs with the Oriental belief that a style that is too hard or too soft touches only half of a person's true nature. Goju claims to have a perfect mixture, thereby enabling one to reach his or her fullest potential in karate.

Tae Kwon Do **Tae kwon do** originated in Korea. The descriptive titles for the movements in this distinct form of karate are still called by their original Korean names. Tae kwon do is somewhat similar to the shotokan style of karate but favors foot and kicking techniques over the use of hand and arm blows.

RANK Your rank in karate is recognized by the uniform belt that you wear. The standard belts in karate, in order of their importance, are: white, green, brown, and black. During recent years, however, other belts have been introduced and added to the traditional ones. Yellow, purple, blue, and red belts are now commonly seen in many dojos. Yellow belts are awarded as the next step up from white. Purple or blue belts are used by some styles of karate to represent a rank between green and brown. The red belt is used in place of the brown belt in some Korean-style schools.

Students of karate are required to pass promotional examinations before they can advance in rank. These qualifying tests are customarily held two or three times each year. High-ranking black belt instructors judge the students according to how well they can demonstrate what they have been taught. Those who are successful are awarded a new belt. This is usually done in the dojo a short while after the official results have been announced. In the event that you fail to be promoted on your first try, don't be discouraged. Your new

belt will have far greater meaning to you when you know that it has been truly earned.

KATA **Kata** is a series of prearranged martial art movements consisting of blocks, strikes, punches, kicks, and stances. There are many different katas in karate, all having varying degrees of difficulty. The higher your rank, the more katas you will be expected to learn. In some styles of karate, katas are a major part of the karate training. It is believed that karate itself would have become a forgotten martial art were it not for the insight of the grand masters in developing these series of movements.

A kata is judged similarly to the routine of a gymnast. In judging, the difficulty of the kata is weighed along with its manner of execution. Some katas last only about one minute. In a perfectly performed kata, the student will start and finish from the same spot and will demonstrate flawless technique. White, yellow, and green belt katas emphasize basic stances, kicks, punches, and blocks. More advanced katas stress breathing, muscular movement and control, power, flexibility, and grace. Katas are an excellent form of exercise. The essence of kata, however, is to defend against an attack in which the movements of your attackers have been previously anticipated. Kata is one aspect of competitive karate where girls and boys com-

This tae kwon do practitioner is demonstrating one of the many moves in the sport.

pete together. The trophies one can win are equally as impressive as those awarded in freestyle competition.

KIAI This is the most misunderstood and difficult facet of karate to explain to the novice student. Some books written on karate state that the **kiai** is a shout used to summon added strength in an attack. This is true, but only partly. The true meaning of kiai originates from two Japanese words, *ki* and *ai*. Ki is a centralized and coordinated form of energy. Ai means integrated harmony of body and mind. In other words, the kiai can concentrate all of one's mental and physical power on a specific target area. It is this discipline that enables the karate practitioner to break boards and even bricks with his or her bare hands. The secret of the amazing martial art of karate is in capturing and controlling this life force energy.

Before you can be ready to learn a kata or practice with another person, you must first become familiar with the basic stances, hand strikes, kicks, and blocks that form the basis of karate.

STANCES Stances are specially designed to develop speed, balance, and maximum power. The most frequently used karate stances are illustrated on page 38.

This martial arts practitioner has summoned all his kiai to break the timber in front of him.

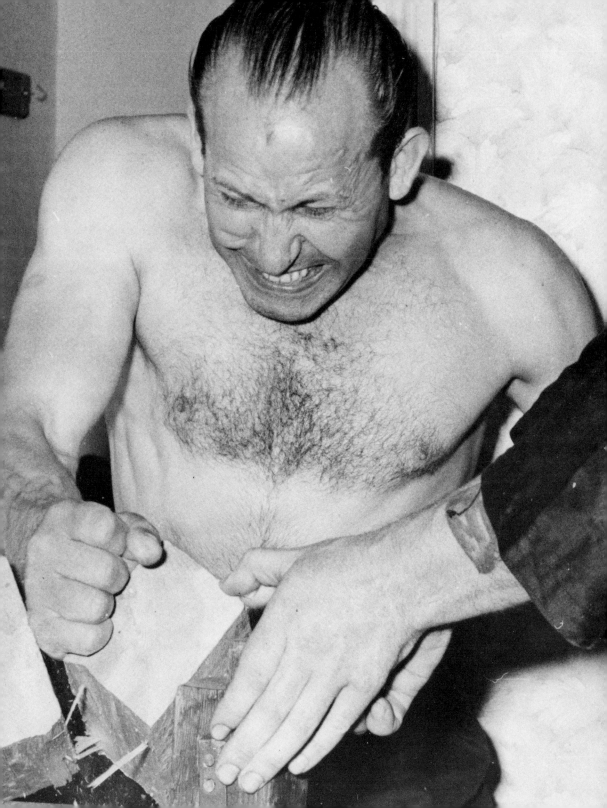

The basic karate stances

HAND STRIKES: The Reverse Punch

The most commonly used strike in karate is the reverse punch. Although it takes time to learn this punch, once you know it you will have an extremely effective weapon. The power of this punch originates from the hip, with help from the shoulder. A famous karate master named Mas Oyama who is still living is credited with having been able to kill bulls with his powerful reverse punch.

The Knifehand Strike

The **knifehand strike,** or chop as it is also called, is probably the most well-known blow in karate. In martial arts demonstrations, the chop is frequently seen as part of board-breaking exhibitions. For practical defense, the knifehand is usually aimed at the neck, temple, or spleen of an attacker. The small bone located just below the wrist reinforces the power of this blow.

Elbow Strikes

The elbow is one of the most durable parts of the human anatomy. A downward or sideward elbow strike by an experienced **karateka** can easily disable an attacker.

The elbow strikes, reverse punch, and other variations of hand blows are shown.

KICKS

Kicking techniques are as important as hand strikes in karate training. A properly executed kick can be an extremely effective weapon. The forebears of the ancient martial art of karate understood the importance of the added reach and strength of the legs in combat. They devised methods of using the legs in blocking certain blows and in sweeping attackers to the ground. In the dojo, as a beginner, you will concentrate most of your time and effort in developing your skill with the

The reverse punch

The knifehand strike

Elbow strikes

SIDE KICK   FRONT KICK

Karate kicks   BACK KICK

**The kick in karate can be
powerful enough to break boards.**

more popular kicking techniques. The manner in which these kicks are used depends upon the direction and nature of the attack.

BLOCKS Blocking is another major component in the art of karate. As with the other movements in karate, students must practice these blocking techniques until they can accomplish them with lightning speed and reflex action. The major blocks are shown here.

TRAINING METHODS In martial arts schools today, the traditional approach is still recognized as the best way of learning karate. In this method of training, the student spends his or her first lessons learning the mechanics of punching, kicking, and blocking as previously described. These techniques are first learned from a natural stance and then tried while in motion. When you can demonstrate sufficient skill and control, you will then be ready to meet face-to-face with an opponent.

One-Step Attack and Defense For this part of the training, the class is usually divided into two lines. Students facing each other are paired off. A threatening real-life situation is improvised as one person in each pair plays the role of an attacker while his or her partner is the defender. In one-step, the attacker must announce how and where he or she intends to attack but does not give any notice as to when the attack will come. The defender must block the attack and counter with a blow of his or her own. This counter-

Karate blocks

INSIDE BLOCK

OUTSIDE BLOCK

UPPER BLOCK

attack must be focused. This means that the blow must show expert technique but be aimed short of the actual target. In this way, students can practice the deadliest karate blows without causing injury to each other. One-step attack and defense is an excellent means of sharpening your reflexes and improving striking and blocking skills. It also prepares you for the next, more difficult practice of semi-freestyle sparring.

Semi-Freestyle Before attempting semi-free sparring, karate players must become totally familiar with the proper methods of moving, blocking, and striking. Again as in one-step, one player attacks while the other defends. In semi-free, however, the attacker is not limited in his or her movements. In this form of sparring the attacker does not tell how or when the attack will take place, only where or to what part of the body the attack is directed.

Freestyle Freestyle is an advanced form of practice and part of competitive tournament karate. In the dojo, the sensei closely supervises this type of practice. In contests, impartial high-ranking instructors serve as referees and judges. When freestyling, either player may attack at will. There is no notice of how, when, or where the other player may attack. The object in this advanced form of practice is to score an ippon (one point) or a **waza-ari** (½ point). In competition the first point awarded determines the winner of each match. A point can be scored only when a focused hit is made to a specified area of the body. This hit must be controlled at the point of contact. When a hit delivered by one player is partially blocked by the other, a waza-ari can be awarded. Today players compete in free-style divisions that are arranged according to the player's rank, weight, and sex.

A Japanese fencing class.

Kendo: "The Way of the Sword"

As recently as two decades ago in Japan, a young kendoist approached his very old teacher to tell him of a dream that recurred in his sleep night after night. In his dream he saw people of all nationalities performing **kendo** around him. The teacher explained that there was profound meaning in this dream but that the young man must search his own soul to find it. The student did as his wise old teacher suggested and afterwards understood that he was being driven by an unknown force to awaken people everywhere to the far-reaching benefits of the sport of kendo.

Before he could have imagined it, the young kendoist was in the United States organizing a kendo club. To his own credit and to the surprise of many skeptics, the club became immediately successful. A short while later, a small kendo dojo was established. As soon as this dojo opened its doors to the public it was overrun with membership requests.

Today, kendo clubs are emerging in cities around the world. It is very possible that because of people like this young man, and the nature of the art itself, kendo will soon rank with judo and karate in world-wide recognition and popularity.

THE ART SWORDS-MANSHIP The first sword was introduced into Japan from China more than a thousand years ago. The art of swordsmanship, originally called **kenjutsu,** dates back to that time. Swords almost immediately replaced other armaments as the most suitable weapons in combat.

The early Japanese swordsmen, called the bushi, were often compared to the crusaders of the middle ages. The European knight, like the bushi, lived by a strict personal code of justice, integrity, and duty. The main difference between the two was in their manner of fighting. While the knight wore a full suit of mail and swung a heavy sword 9 feet (2.7 m) in length, the bushi preferred freedom of movement and carried a sword only half the size of his legendary European counterpart. The bushi would face his opponent squarely in the front, with his feet firmly planted on the ground and his eyes staring coldly into the eyes of his enemy. His sword, when drawn, would thrash out with lightning speed in a "ground-to-sky" motion. From this basic approach, many **ryu,** or styles of **fencing,** developed.

THE STYLES OF SWORDPLAY While no one can say with absolute certainty who was the best fencer of all time, a few have stood apart from all the rest. These magnificent master swordsmen gained reputations that followed them wherever they went. Each was recognized by his own unique manner of using his sword. Lesser-skilled swordsmen tried to copy the methods used by their favorite champion. In this way the various styles of kenjutsu developed.

EARLY METHODS OF TRAINING

When a soldier was called upon to use his sword in battle, there was no margin for error allowed. Unlike the unarmed methods of combat, the slightest mistake in fencing could prove fatal. No method of training could therefore be too thorough, for the bushi's life depended upon his preparedness.

The training methods subscribed to by the masters of kenjutsu were designed to discourage all but the most dedicated students. The **bokken** was the main instrument of training. Fashioned after the open-blade sword, the bokken was almost equal in size and weight but was made of hard wood instead of steel. Although a blow from this wooden sword was seldom fatal, it could nevertheless inflict serious injury. In this way the masters of kenjutsu copied as closely as they could real-life combat situations. The seriousness with which this study was taken was further evidenced by the fact that no protective equipment was ever allowed to be worn during practice.

THE TRANSITION FROM KENJUTSU TO KENDO

During the age of the great swordsmen lived a creative thinker and skilled fencer—by the name of Chuta Nakanishi. Chuta hoped to one day open a fencing hall of his own, for he believed that he could improve upon the then most popular method of teaching. He was certain that the hazardous training methods that were being used were restricting the students' ability to learn. By removing the fear and risk of injury, Chuta contended that one could more freely practice the art of swordsmanship.

Chuta's first significant step forward in this direction came with his invention of the **shinai,** or bamboo fencing foil. This lightweight practice sword was well made but not nearly as dangerous as the bokken. As the value of the shinai was first being realized, Chuta introduced another new piece of fencing equipment called the **kote,** or protective glove.

Some of the older senseis frowned upon these changes in the customary approach to teaching, but most appreciated the advantages of these new implements. In fact, later masters expanded upon Nakanishi's idea by developing further protective equipment. Along these lines, the **tare** was introduced to afford the fencer ample protection from a low attack aimed to the hip or groin. The tare was heavily padded and was tied around at the waist. The next piece of protective equipment to be introduced was the **do,** or chest protector, which was constructed from strips of bamboo and covered with leather hide. The **men,** or head, face, and neck mask, was designed to prevent injury to that part of the body. This was an advanced piece of fencing gear that included a steel faceguard with flaps extending to the lower neck area.

By using this new equipment, a fencer could practice full-force striking and thrusting movements in the dojo without fear of the consequences to an opponent. As Chuta Nakanishi envisioned, this proved to be of great value in training. However, not even he could have imagined the far greater consequence of his invention of the bamboo sword! His shinai and the other protective equipment was to form the basis of a new sport, the martial art of kendo.

KENDO STRATEGY

The samurai would never draw his sword unless compelled to do so, but on these occasions he would hold nothing back. In modern kendo, players are taught in this traditional manner to aim their shinais at the most vulnerable parts of the body. All kendo strikes must be directed to one of the recognized target areas. These areas are, namely, the upper part of the head, the throat, the sides of the body, and the wrists. When aiming to the throat, the **tsuki,** or lunging thrust is used. All other blows in the sport of kendo are slicing or cutting strikes called **kiri.** The preferred attack of most kendoists is the downward kiri to the head.

When the kendoist moves, his or her steps are fast and gliding. When counterattacking, he or she may also jump forward upon the opponent in order to gain optimum power in the attack. This jump sometimes also frightens an opponent into dropping his or her guard. In kendo, players are constantly watchful for these openings. During practice sessions students are taught how to distract their opponents. At the moment the opponent has lost his or her concentration, the student launches the attack. To truly test your ability in kendo you must compete in a formal duel with another experienced kendoist.

THE KENDO MATCH

When two kendoists face one another in a tournament match, they first bow according to the age-old cus-

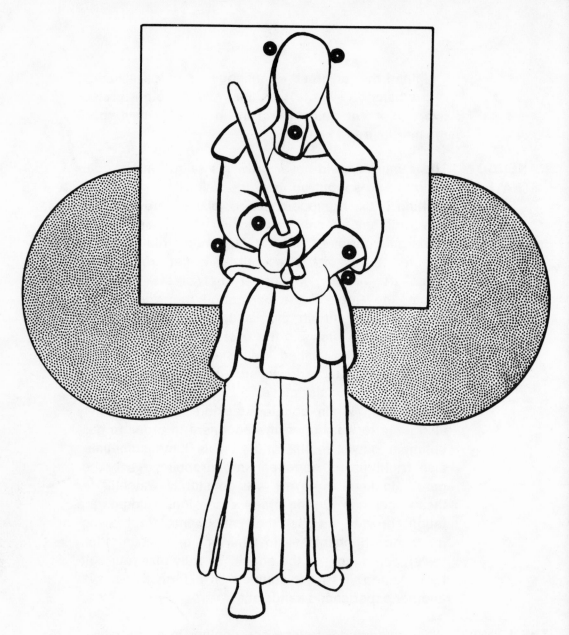

Above: the kendo target areas.
Right: a kendo match.

toms of etiquette and respect among opponents. The contestants then assume an on-guard position called **maai.** When the word **hajime** is heard the match begins. For the next several minutes both players try to score points by affecting a clean hit to any one of the eight target areas.

The rules of the match dictate that the first player to score two hits be declared the winner. That player then earns the right to challenge another player of equal rank. This round-robin elimination continues until there remains but one undefeated player in each division.

PRESENT POPULARITY OF KENDO

Many who begin studying kendo enjoy it so very much that they never grow tired of learning more about it. In Japan, kendo is a national sport. Students can, if they choose, study kendo in junior high or high school. On the university level, many scholarships are awarded to superior fencers.

Kendo competition is no longer limited to the Orient. The United States, Britain, and Brazil are but a few of the countries that presently hold national kendo championships. People are talking more and more lately about the lifelong benefits of kendo in building character and enhancing physical and mental well-being. The day when kendo gains recognition by the International Olympic Committee may be very close at hand.

Aikido

Aikido is a weaponless means of fighting derived from **bujutsu,** an ancient Japanese warring art. Aikido has been called the ultimate method of self-defense, for it employs only defensive maneuvers and techniques. In the martial art of aikido, there are no provisions for attacking or counterattacking. In many ways, an aikido master can be compared to a great escape artist. Both train endlessly for the moment when they must use their skills to escape danger. Each of them also places much importance upon the workings of the body joints. By learning how to manipulate another person's body joints, the aikidoist gains the ability to redirect the opponent's movements. In this way the aikido practitioner, when attacked, can miraculously escape injury.

HOW AIKIDO WAS FOUNDED Morei Uyeshiba, who was born in Japan during the latter part of the nineteenth century, was the founder

of aikido. Morei never cared much for wealth, power, or fame. He was a simple and humble man who had but one great desire—to learn all he could about the martial arts. To achieve his goal, he would travel throughout the countryside in search of the most highly respected champions in all the land. Some of the masters with whom Uyeshiba was privileged to study with died without ever revealing their secrets to anyone other than Uyeshiba.

Among the many and varied martial art forms that Morei learned were jiujitsu and **jijutsu** (unarmed combat), **yarijutsu** (spear fighting), kendo (fencing), and **kyudo** (archery). In addition to his extensive physical training, Uyeshiba also sought spiritual guidance in understanding the true essence of the martial arts. One day, while he was meditating near a holy refuge, he discovered that the study of the martial arts helped one learn how to live with others in harmony. This inspired him to develop aikido, a superior fighting form that could only be used in self-defense.

THE FIRST AIKIDO DOJO   Master Uyeshiba introduced his novel martial art to the Japanese people by opening his own school in metropolitan Tokyo. His methods aroused much interest in the highest circles of martial arts enthusiasts everywhere. People who were themselves highly skilled in other fighting forms enrolled in his school. The praise he received from other grand masters won him

A class in aikido.

worldwide acclaim. Although aikido is admittedly not the simplest martial art to learn, there is no longer any doubt as to its remarkable effectiveness.

HOW AIKIDO WORKS

The aikido disciple endeavors to use knowledge and skill to teach an aggressor a lesson in humanity rather than to cause pain or injury. It is believed that only by the defender reacting in a more humane way than the attacker can the cycle of violence be broken.

The aikido student's first lessons are taken up learning the easiest and least harmful methods of escaping from various holds. Following this, the pupil learns how to avoid a variety of punches and strikes aimed at all parts of the body. During the next step in the technical training, methods of **immobilizations** are learned. As the name suggests, in these types of techniques the aikido practitioner learns how to momentarily stop the opponent's movements. Finally, the aikidoist learns **projections,** or ways of using the wrist and elbow joints as well as the attacker's own movements to throw him or her to the ground. The illustrations show some of the holds from which the aikido participant learns how to escape and also various immobilizations and projections used. To understand the principle of misdirecting an opponent's force, one of the major components in the art of aikido, try this. First, have a friend grab both your arms at the wrists to try to pre-

The aikido basic holds

Some immobilizations and projections

FRONT APPROACH BODY THROW

CONTROL MOVEMENT

ELBOW LOCK

vent them from moving. Now, move your arms sideward and outward away from your body. Next, throw your arms quickly in an inward and upward motion, as if you were hitching a ride. You will notice that your friend's grip has loosened. This occurs because force can only be exerted in one direction at a time.

"May the force always be with you!"

AIKIDO: THE ULTIMATE MARTIAL ART

Because aikido emphasizes agility and precision before strength and force, it is considered an ideal activity for the young. To be successful at aikido, it isn't necessary that you be tall or have a powerful build. It is more important that you be able to move swiftly and gracefully. Aikido has been called the most gentle of the martial arts because of its noncombative nature and design. As there are few, if any, striking, grabbing, pulling, or pushing movements in aikido, accidental injuries are also rare. The training involved in learning aikido skills will also prove very useful when playing sports that require pinpoint timing and excellent body coordination. Boys and girls who study dancing, tumbling, and gymnastics have displayed a noticeable improvement in their performance in these activities as a result of the excellent balance and body control learned in aikido practice. Moreover, certain exercises in aikido have been proven effective in promoting general health and may even help in curing many types of physical ailments. These refined characteristics of aikido make it the most highly sophisticated and most generally desirable of all the martial arts. This is why many people often refer to aikido as the "ultimate" martial art.

Kung Fu

Of the many and varied martial art forms, none has been guarded with greater secrecy than the Chinese art of **kung fu.** The masters of this ancient fighting form were, according to unwritten law, forbidden to teach their skills to any non-Chinese person. This rule, which also applied to other Oriental nationalities, was kept in force for countless centuries. It wasn't until as recently as the year 1964 when this tradition was finally broken. In that year, for the first time ever, a kung-fu **sifu** (teacher) opened the doors of his **kwoon** (school) to people of all races. Master Wong Ark Yuey had at the time no idea of the full impact of his decision: Kung fu was destined to soon become the marvel of martial arts followers everywhere.

THE ART OF KUNG FU   Kung fu, or **wu-shu** as it was originally known, is the oldest of all the martial arts studied today. The fascination of kung fu (also pronounced gong-fu and known as hung chuen in China and tong chuen in Okinawa) comes from the myths and legends that followed the Chinese Taoist priests who first developed wu-shu. These early practitioners supposedly acquired supernatural abilities from their lifelong dedication to the study of their sheltered art. According to ancient Chinese belief, there is an inner life force contained inside each one of us that is capable of elevating a person toward the accomplishment of things normally thought impossible. Kung fu teaches how to harness this inner life force and how to make meaningful use of it in one's daily life.

KUNG FU: FACT AND FICTION

For many years, the classical art of kung fu was associated with stories about the "iron hand" and the elusive "poison touch of death." As the words suggest, iron hand was supposed to be a fist possessing iron-like strength and power. The so-called poison or death touch referred to the ability the kung-fu master supposedly had to kill an enemy with just the slightest touch of his finger. It was even told that some grand masters had the power to cause the pain of a blow to be felt moments or even hours after the initial strike was inflicted, a phenomenon known as deferred injury. Because there exists no absolute way to disprove the validity of these tales, they have remained with us until the present. Most students of kung-fu today, however, believe that the iron hand is no more than a hand that is hardened and calloused by rigorous physical conditioning. They also believe there is no such thing as a death touch or any way to cause deferred injury. There remains, however, enough fascination in the real art of kung fu to make these students want to give up many other enjoyable activities and devote much of their spare time toward learning its treasured secrets.

THE TREASURED SECRETS OF KUNG FU

The founders of kung fu incorporated into their fighting form much of what was then known about the human anatomy and traditional methods of healing. In ancient China, two major methods were used in the treatment of physical ailments. One of these methods involved the use of herbs in aiding digestion. From this evolved the science of pharmaceutical medicine. The other method of healing employed by the Chinese sages involved the control of pain by applying pressure to vital nerves of the body. From this evolved the branch of medical science called **acupressure.** The founding fathers of wu-shu, who were themselves skilled in these arts, developed ways to use their knowledge of pressure points and vital nerve areas for self-defense.

STYLES OF KUNG FU

The movements of kung fu are believed to have been patterned after the movements of wild animals. The animals that most particularly influenced the development of kung fu were birds, bears, monkeys, tigers, and deer. It was, the Taoist priests observed, the strength and speed of the big cat that enabled it to so easily overpower the largest and heaviest jungle animals. The monkey, on the other hand, had the uncanny ability to distract and deceive its natural enemies. From the actions of birds such as the crane was learned the talent of winging and hooking a foe. The deer's

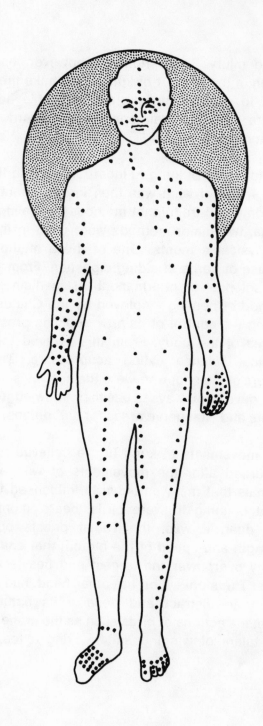

ability to jump and kick protected its species from the ever-present dangers of the wild. As for the bear, it was the use of its claws that impressed the early disciples. These actions were studied and imitated and eventually formed the basic movements of kung fu. The theory of vital pressure points, the use of organic potents, and the belief that proper breathing is related to good health all also became incorporated into kung fu teachings. The degree of emphasis placed upon each of these elements varied. The result was the emergence of hundreds of different styles of kung fu. Many of these styles have recently incorporated into the art of kung-fu training other methods of armed defense.

BRUCE LEE: THE MAN WITH THREE LEGS

There was no martial arts personality better known or more admired than the late Bruce Lee. During his brief but eventful lifetime, Lee made a greater contribution than perhaps all who preceded him in promoting the study of martial arts and most particularly the ancient art of kung fu. Although he held no formal rank or belt (ranks and belts are not awarded in kung fu), he was nevertheless a model practitioner of kung fu from his early youth. During martial arts exhibitions, he would dazzle audiences with his amazing quickness. This led to his famous nickname, "the man with three legs."

The pressure points utilized in kung fu.

Bruce Lee's performances on these occasions aroused the interest of a wide variety of people, including some famous Hollywood film producers. Soon Bruce was on his way to becoming a star. His films were overnight box-office sensations. Kung fu was suddenly the most talked about fighting form and Bruce Lee its most famous practitioner. Then Bruce was suddenly taken ill and died. His death was mourned by millions of fans who by that time spanned the globe.

**The renowned Bruce Lee
in his film,
*The Chinese Connection.***

Martial Arts Associations

JUDO   International Judo Federation
70 Brompton Road
London, S.W. 3 1 Drive
England

United States Judo Federation
Route 1, Box 519
Terre Haute, Indiana 47802

KARATE   All-American Karate Federation
1440 West Olympic Boulevard
Los Angeles, California 90034

International Amateur Karate Federation
1440 West Olympic Boulevard
Los Angeles, California 90034

United Karate Federation
139 East 56th Street
New York, New York 10022

AIKIDO U.S. Aikido Federation
142 West 18th Street
New York, New York 10011

Los Angeles Aiki Kai
8929 Ellis Avenue
Los Angeles, California 90034

KENDO Kendo Federation of the United States of America
1715 West 256th Street
Lomita, California 90717

Glossary and Pronunciation Guide

Acupressure An Oriental medical science that treats physical maladies through the application of pressure to vital body organs.

Aikido [eye-KEY-doe] The "gentleman's" fighting form. In aikido, the least harmful and most ethical means of defense are taught.

Bojitsu [boe-JIT-sue] The ancient Oriental art of fighting using long wooden staffs as weapons.

Bokken [BOW-kin] The wooden sword from which later evolved the modern fencing foil.

Bujutsu [boo-JUT-sue] The name given to the many ancient warrior arts of old Japan.

Bushido [boo-SHE-doe] A code of conduct of old Japan that is still followed to some extent in the more traditional dojos.

Dan [dan] This word pertains to the level of excellence reached by the expert practitioners of the martial arts.

Death touch The supposed ability of kung-fu masters to kill with just a touch of their hand.

Do [doe] The do is the chest piece worn in the art of kendo. Once purchased, the do never needs replacement.

Dojo [DOE-joe]   A training hall where the various martial arts are taught.

Fencing   Activity in which swords are used for sport or recreation and their use is restricted by a set of rules.

Gi [gee]   A martial arts uniform. Gis vary slightly, depending on the form practiced. The belt that is tied around the gi symbolizes the level of expertise the student has gained.

Goju [GO-jew]   The "hard and soft" style of karate.

Grand Masters   Holy men whose religious training was tied to the study of martial arts principles.

Hajime [ha-gee-MAY]   The word used to signal the start of an official contest or match.

Immobilizations   Situations in which an aikido player is able to lock the other player's body joints and thereby stop his or her movements altogether.

Ippon [ee-PON]   A point in martial arts competition.

Jijutsu [gee-JUT-sue]   The name for the ancient unarmed warrior arts.

Jiujitsu [gee-oo-JIT-sue]   The martial art form that most influenced the formation of the sport of judo.

Judo [JEW-doe]   Known as the gentle or flexible way, judo is today the most recognized of all martial arts.

Judogi [JEW-doe-gee]   Full name for the judo gi, or uniform outfit worn in judo.

Judoka [jew-DOE-ka]   Refers to all judo players, beginner through expert.

Karate [ka-RAH-tay]   The emptyhanded art of unarmed combat now performed in every major city in the world for fun and for self-defense.

Karateka [kah-RAH-teek-kah]   A practitioner of karate.

Kata [CAUGHT-ah]   A dance-like routine that demonstrates the movements of a particular martial art.

Kendo   A Japanese sport patterned after the sword movements of the samurai warriors of feudal Japan.

Kenjutsu [ken-JUT-sue]   The ancient art of the "open blade," or steel-edged sword.

Kiai [KEY-eye]   A shout that increases body energy and power.

Kimono [key-MOW-no]   A long and loose-fitting silk robe.

Kiri [KEY-a-ree]   The chopping and slicing movements that form the basic techniques of Japanese fencing.

Knifehand strike   Also called the chop, this is the most publicized blow in karate, which often results in a board or a brick being broken in half.

Kodokan [KOE-doe-con]   The first judo dojo, which was started by the founder of the sport, Dr. Jigoro Kano. The Kodokan is still in existence today and is the largest martial arts facility in the world.

Kote [KOE-tay]   The glove used in kendo for hand, wrist, and forearm protection.

Kung fu [kung-FOO]   The so-called classical art of self-defense, fashioned after the instinctive behavior of animals engaged in battle with other animals. Also considered by some a form of karate.

Kuzushi [koo-ZOO-she]   The ability to off-balance an opponent while maintaining your own balance.

Kwoon   The practice or training hall where the art of kung fu is learned.

Kyu [cue]   A rank between beginner and black belt in judo. The lower the kyu number, the higher the rank. After reaching 1st kyu, a player may try for black-belt ranking.

Kyudo [key-EU-doe]   An ancient martial art form similar to archery.

Maai [mee]   The distance or space separating two kendoists at the start of a match.

Martial Arts   Competitive sports and activities designed for general health and self-defense.

Mattai [MAT-tie]   A word frequently heard in judo contests meaning, "Let go, I give up."

Meiji [MEE-gee]   The name of the government in Japan that held power from 1868 to 1912. The Meiji Edict of 1878 banned the use of swords in public places.

Men [men]   The heavy steel faceguard used in the martial art of kendo.

Nage waza   Throwing techniques used in judo.

Newaza Methods of hold-downs, armlocks, and chokes used in the art of judo.

Okinawa The island that gave birth to many schools of Oriental combat and promoted the study of the unarmed martial arts.

Projections When the force of an attacker is used to throw him or her to the ground. Most often heard when referring to the art of aikido.

Randori [ran-DOOR-ee] When two players compete in a practice match, with each testing the other's skills to the limit.

Rei [ree] The act of bowing, Japanese style, or the command to bow.

Ryu [rue] The styles of fencing that developed around the invention of the samurai sword.

Samurai [SAM-or-eye] The knights of old Japan who measured their lives not in years but in deeds. Also known as the bushi.

Sensei [SEN-say] An expert teacher of one or more of the marital arts.

Shaolin-Szu [SHAY-o-lin-zoo] An ancient Chinese monastery that gained fame as the first institution to promote the study of martial arts disciplines.

Shiai [SHE-eye] A match in competitive judo.

Shihan [SHE-han] A judo master.

Shinai [SHEEN-eye] The practice sword used in kendo that is constructed from lightweight and durable bamboo cane.

Shotokan [SHOW-toe-kan] A "point blank" style of karate that emphasizes speed, power, and controlled force.

Sifu [SEE-foo] The kung fu master.

Sparring A part of martial arts training that permits the students to test their skills in simulated combat situations.

Tae kwon do [tay-kwon-DOE] A Korean karate style that makes optimum use of the legs in combat.

Tare [TAR-ree] The waist and hip protector used in the martial art of kendo.

Tori [TOR-ree] The aggressor in the sport of judo.

Tsuki [ZOO-key] A heavy cotton flap used in kendo to protect the neck and throat. Tsuki also means a sword thrust to those areas of the body.

Uchikomi [oo-KEM-ee] A method of judo practice whereby players apply controlled resistance.

Uke [youk] The player who acts as an assistant to another trying to learn a new movement or technique.

Ukemi [you-KEY-mee] Methods of falling learned in judo that help in minimizing the impact of falls.

Waza-ari [wa-za-AR-ee] A score (½ point) awarded for the execution of a near-perfect technique in freestyle or freeform karate competition.

Wu-shu [WOO-shoe] The original Chinese name for the ancient art of kung fu.

Yarijutsu [ya-ree-JUT-sue] One of the less popular martial arts involving the use of spears in self-defense.

Zen Buddhism A Chinese and later Japanese school of Buddhism, which stresses the benefits of contemplation and meditation.

Books for Further Reading

Bartlett, E. G. *Basic Judo.* Photos. New York: Arco Publishing Co., 1975.

Bruce, Jeannette. *Judo—A Gentle Beginning.* Illustrated. New York: Thomas Y. Crowell, 1975.

Corcoran, John and Farkas, Emil. *The Complete Martial Arts Catalogue.* Photos. New York: Simon and Schuster, 1977.

Draegar, Donn F. and Smith, Robert W. *Asian Fighting Arts.* Illustrated. New York: Berkley Publishing, 1974.

Harrison, E. J. *Junior Judo.* Illustrated. New York: Archway Paperbacks, 1977.

Masters, Robert V. *The Complete Book of Karate and Self-Defense.* Photos. New York: Sterling Publishing Co., 1974.

Oyama, Masutatsu. *Boy's Karate.* Illustrated. Elmsford, N.Y.: Japan Publications, 1969.

Tegner, Bruce. *Kung Fu and Tai Chi*. Photos. Ventura, Calif.: Thor Publishing, 1973.

Warner, Gordon, and Sasamori, Junzo. *This is Kendo: The Art of Japanese Fencing*. Illustrated. Rutland, Vt.: Charles E. Tuttle, 1964.

Westbrook, A. and Ratti, O. *Aikido and the Dynamic Sphere*. Illustrated. Rutland, Vt.: Charles E. Tuttle, 1970.

Index

About the Author

Ken Reisberg currently works in
the field of housing management.
In his spare time he writes books
for young readers, including the just-
published *Card Games* (A First Book)
for Franklin Watts, and participates
in a number of hobbies and sports.
Ken studied the martial art of
karate as a child and received a
brown belt in it.

Ken makes his home in Brooklyn,
New York. He has a wife, Doris,
and a son named Ivan.